Ghost Station

SUE HUBBARD is a freelance art critic, lecturer, novelist and poet. Her first poetry collection *Everything Begins with the Skin* was published by Enitharmon in 1994. Twice winner of the London Writers competition and a winner of a number of other major prizes, her work has appeared in The Observer and The Independent, as well as in numerous anthologies and been broadcast on Radio 4. The Poetry Society's first ever Public Art Poet she worked in Birmingham to create a series of site-specific poems in the jewellery quarter and was commissioned by the Arts Council and the BFI to write London's biggest public art poem, *Euridyce* at The South Bank. In 2002 she was writer-in-residence at The De La Warr Pavilion, Bexhill-on-Sea.

A regular columnist for The Independent she has written for Time Out, The New Statesman, The Independent on Sunday, Contemporary, Tate, Art Review and The RA magazine. The founder member of Writers inc., she also teaches creative writing at the Royal College of Art, has taught at Arvon and run workshops at Tate Britain.

Twenty of her poems appeared in *Oxford Poets 2000*, published by Carcanet, which won a PBS Recommendation.

Her first novel *Depth of Field* was published in spring 2000 by Dewi Lewis. John Berger called it "a remarkable first novel."

Other publications by the same author

Poetry
I dreamt I remembered what love was (Priapus Press, 1987)
Venetian Red (Hearing Eye, 1993)
Everything Begins with the Skin (Enitharmon, 1994)
Opening Spaces: poetry as Public Art (Poetry Society Publication, as part of Poetry Society's Poetry Places scheme funded by the 'Arts for Everyone' budget of the Arts Council of England's Lottery Department.)

Novel
Depth of Field (Dewi Lewis, 2000)

Ghost Station

Sue Hubbard

PUBLISHED BY SALT PUBLISHING
PO Box 937, Great Wilbraham, Cambridge PDO CB1 5JX United Kingdom
PO Box 202, Applecross, Western Australia 6153

© Sue Hubbard, 2004

The right of Sue Hubbard to be identified as the
author of this work has been asserted by her in accordance
with Section 77 of the Copyright, Designs and Patents Act 1988.

First published 2004

Printed and bound in the United Kingdom by Lightning Source

Typeset in Swift 9.5 / 13

ISBN 1 84471 035 1 paperback

SP

1 3 5 7 9 8 6 4 2

For Tim
who could not make sense of it all

Contents

Acknowledgments

Nude in Bathtub won third prize in the Cardiff Competition and was published in The Observer and Oxford Poets 2000. *Eurydice* was commissioned by the BFI and The Arts Council as part of the regeneration of the South Bank. *Ghost Station* won third prize in the National Poetry Competition 2000 and was previously shortlisted in the TLS/Blackwells Competition and was published in The Independent. *Stereoptica, Dolls* and *Bat* were first published in London Magazine. *Rooms* was first published in The Dybbuk of Delight. *Woodcuts, Alchemies, Room in New York, Border, Gone to Earth, Books, Christmas* and *Darwin's Worms* were first published in Oxford Poets 2000. *Hotel* (also published in Oxford Poets) was first commissioned by Brass Art for their catalogue Stalk. *Loss* (also published in Oxford Poets) *Moths* and *Page* were first published in Poetry London. *Sheen, Toad* and *The Sower* were first published in In the Company of Poets, Hearing Eye. *Porth Levan* was first published in Acumen. *Autumn Rhythm* was first published in The Observer. *Gone to Earth* and *Rope* won first prize in the London Writers Competition 1999 and 2002.

Thanks is due to the Hawthornden Foundation, to the Yaddo Foundation and The Tyrone Gutherie Centre where a number of these poems were written.

Also to the artist Albert Duplock whose woodcuts were the inspiration for the series of that name, to Alice Maher, whose photographs inspired *Metamorphosis* and to Mario Petrucci, Philip Gross, Michael Hulse and Jules Smith who all commented, at some stage, on these poems.

"And so we keep pressing on, trying to achieve it,
trying to hold it firmly in our simple hands,
in our overcrowded gaze, in our speechless hearts."
RILKE

"Some have a great dream in life, and fall short of it.
Others have no dream, and also fall short of it."
FERNANDO PESSOA

Stereotopica

Nude in Bathtub

After Bonnard

Between the edge of the afternoon
and dusk, between the bath's white
rim and the band of apricot light,
she bathed, each day, as if dreaming.

From the doorway he noted
her right foot hooked for balance
beneath the enamel lip, body
and water all one in a miasma

of mist, a haze of lavender blue.
Such intimacy. A woman, two walls,
a chequered floor, the small
curled dog basking in a pool

of sun reflected from the tiles
above the bath. Outside
the throbbing heat. So many times
he has drawn her, caught the obsessive

soaping of her small breasts,
compressed the crouched frame into
his picture space, the nervy movements
that hemmed in his life.

The house exudes her still,
breathes her from each sunlit corner,
secretes her lingering smell
from shelves of rosewood *armoires,*

and the folded silk *chemises*
he doesn't have the heart to touch.
And from the landing, his memory tricks,
as through the open door the smudged

floor glistens with silvered tracks,
her watered foot prints to and from
the tub where she floats in almond oil
deep in her sarcophagus of light.

Eurydice

I am not afraid as I descend,
    step by step, leaving behind the salt wind
        blowing up the corrugated river,

the damp city streets, their sodium glare
    of rush-hour headlights pitted with pearls of rain;
        for my eyes still reflect the half-remembered moon.

Already your face recedes beneath the station clock,
    a damp smudge among the shadows
        mirrored in the train's wet glass.

Will you forget me? Steel tracks lead you out
    past cranes and crematoria,
        boat yards and bike sheds, ruby shards

of Roman glass and wolf-bone mummified in mud,
    the rows of curtained windows like eyelids heavy
        with sleep, to the city's green edge.

Now I stop my ears with wax, hold fast
    the memory of the song you once whispered in my ear.
        Its echoes tangle like briars in my thick hair.

You turned to look . . .
    Seconds fly past like birds.
        My hands grow cold. I am ice and cloud.

This path unravels.
    Deep in hidden rooms filled with dust
        and sour-night breath the lost city is sleeping.

Above, the hurt sky is weeping,
   soaked nightingales have ceased to sing.
      Dusk has come too early. I am drowning in blue.

I dream of a green garden
   where the sun feathers my face
      like your once eager kiss.

Soon, soon I will climb
   from this blackened earth
      into the diffident light.

Ghost Station

Rosslyn

Wild garlic and rain in the woods and between invisible tracks
that lead from here to there I sense them glide
through their lost narratives down platforms of damps ferns.

Think of a bent hair-pin lodged for years under a wooden carriage seat
fallen from a stook of auburn hair, a single collar-stud trapped beneath
the floor that once fastened small intimacies behind a film of beaded glass,

or an old man's knotted hand, knuckles raw in the niche of his lap
carrying home a gift of speckled eggs. Imagine the pallor of rain
ashen, pewter, stained watery-sheen along a backbone of glinting steel,

and shadows of coal-dust, steam and sparks on iron where green tongues
of larkspur grow. Turn your head and glimpse between verticals of larch
and beech blotched autobiographies like smudged footprints in wet grass.

Listen, where the wind throws back its dialogue of despair behind
the raindrops, acknowledges lives drained away, like a plume
of smoke recalled along invisible tracks by a damp bird's solitary song.

Stereoptica

They did not know, inhabiting their real skins, unconscious
of the moment's true currency they would be frozen as history:
the bell-boy with the band-box hat set slightly askew posing
by Landseer's lion in Trafalgar Square or the woman hurrying
along the cobble strand by Tower Bridge under a silk parasol,

the heliotropic tilt of her head leaning in towards her
two daughters, hair in braids under boaters of straw.
How could these tea gatherers, young girls bent
like saplings under the overseers' brutal gaze beneath
the weight of panniers in the blue hills near *Galle* in old Ceylon,

or the grizzled traders – twigs of mahogany in white *dhotis* –
in the dirt street below the Madura Pagoda in 1893,
know that a palm-slip of silver, the morning's weighing
of saffron or rice would be preserved like those
albino babies in filmy jars on dark museum shelves labelled

in Indian ink? Or that from these erased histories,
I could, through this lensed *masque*, like Lazarus, make them rise
from their matt solitude – not themselves, but something
of themselves – freed momentarily from bleached effacement,
like damp-winged moths ascending ephemeral in evening air.

Portrait of Woman in a Blue Tunic
Roman period c.AD 160–70

They gave her a painted face to welcome death,
a nip-and-tuck in encaustic fit for eternity:
hieratic blush of madder and white lead,
coiled hair in warm Japan.

Behind the sophistication of coifed curls,
those earstuds of malachite and pearls,
the plaque of carnelian in the dip of her throat
she stares out full of quiet restraint,

as though she had reined something wounded in.
No meticulous archaeology discovered her,
just the illegal grubbings
of Theodar Graf, antiquities dealer

with an instinct for a kill,
riffling the hot sands of Fauym and er-Rubayat,
dreaming at night of pale Victorian girls.
I am pleased that he found her.

I've been carrying around this museum postcard
for days, struggling to hold her olive-black gaze
across two millennia, trying to interpret
the hieroglyphs of death's silent grammar,

as if she'd simply slipped –
hair shining in lamplight –
through a gap in the impermanence of things
to call me away from this visible skin.

Rooms

Out beyond the half-shadows
of silent rooms where dust
collects between the keys
of unplayed pianos, gathers
along hidden picture rails
and coats in a willow-pattern
bowl, greying cubes of sugar,

out beyond the lamp-light,
the yoked rim seeping
cinnamon rings onto Persian
rugs and the smeared glass,
past the crabbed cherry,
the lavender and mint,
the barbs of rosemary
and pots of withered balm,

past the privet and the creosoted
fence where embers flicker
like baited breath among
piles of sodden leaves
and the smell of wood-smoke
rises in October air
catching the nostrils,

beyond these there is only
something felt, something
inaudible, an impossible
longing rising in a plume
of wood-smoke beyond the hedge
and herb garden, the lamp-light,
like dust settling between
the cracks of floor-boards,
coating the forgotten sugar.

Dolls

Bethnal Green Museum of Childhood

Beneath velvet bonnets
they have ringlets of real hair,
painted eyes that stare

and stare in periwinkle blue.
Their cherry lips are chipped,
cracks craze their bisque faces.

Ruched and frilled they sit on glass
shelves starched and prinked in stained
lawn pinafores endlessly pouring tea.

But they will not tell. Will hold fast
their secrets beneath percale and pink
foulard, dumb witnesses to those cold

nursery fears. Downstairs: lights, oranges,
a Viennese waltz ... in her window-seat
the beaded sweat of glass.

Lulled by laudanum she hugs the limp
cloth-body to petticoats and shift, in cambric
shadows reaches for a cool china hand.

Faces

Travelling up to London from the coast by train
after days of rain,
fields have become lakes, lakes inland seas.
Midday is
brindled twilight and in the smeared glass my face doubles,
a pale spectre
coming towards me across soaked hedgerows and fields.
And in an instant
I am back on those dark stairs huddled behind
oak banisters
where wisteria presses witchy profiles against the window panes
as ancient plumbing
gurgles through the guts of the house and the hushed harshness
of adult voices rises
like the odour of chrysanthemums from the
Waterford vase
that surely means divorce, an orphanage;
or shut in with those elfin faces
leering from the black and white squares of mottled bathroom
linoleum
that will get me if I open my eyes or don't finish
peeing before
the count of twenty and pull my knickers quickly
up over scraped knees
to run, without even washing my hands, to the safety
of my bedroom.

Piano

She remembers that cold room,
her father's photo, stone thumbs,
glass fingers brittle as frost,

the music like a ribbon of blood
opening and opening the locked
ventricles of her swollen heart

minims, crochets, semibreves
ragged crows that refused to take flight,
disparity of dreaming and will . . .

In the cobwebbed corner
it sits hunkered in shadows
of sunlight, closed lid

a polished lip to hold
lemon balm, the framed photos
of grown children.

A clock ticks.
Curtains lift, pale birds,
in the afternoon wind.

Moths

For weeks she has known they
are in there. The furred flutterings
between escarpments of wool,
folded crevices of blankets.

Spring she sprinkled snowballs
of camphor, but still, behind
closed doors imagines clouds
of wood-brown wings beating

between the hills and hummocks
of outgrown sweaters, mandibles
shredding their discarded winter warmth.
All summer they must have hatched

in the fierce heat, now slub-laced motes
slip like dust behind her eyelids,
flit across her tea-coloured dreams.
She will not open the cupboard,

let them out to whirr in curtains
and hair towards the bright light
of vacant bedrooms. Again
she will turn away to polish taps,

water the lemon balm,
leave for another day the pale
featherings unravelling her satin trims.

Darwin's Worms

En masse, they were, he realised,
the earth's natural geologists, noted how
a piece of drained marl

harrowed then ploughed
by the heavy tread of feathered cobs
would disclose beneath its fine tilth,

the soft mulch of vegetable decay,
blue shards of pottery, splinters of ivory bone
ejected at the mouth of casts.

He studied their hermaphrodite matings,
recorded how their work was carried out
hidden beneath the surface geest or at night

under a wet moon as their pink bodies
wandered digesting and ejecting the triturated earth.
All life, he now saw, was informed

by loss, each micro-second
a brief stay against erasure
before invisibility set in.

And then he understood
how he must relinquish redemption,
learn to let time heal and pass,

for what was divinity if it could only come
with a wing-beat of angels?
And in his mind's eye he glimpsed

the grand collaboration, the earth
transformed by their inexhaustible work, reborn
again and again though the intestines of worms.

The Sower
Jean-Francois Millet 1850

Thighs braced against the curve
of field, puddled armpits
rancid in the freezing wind
he strides

diagonally down the slope
beneath a weight of sky.
From behind the ridge
the low sun catches

his left cheek, his hand, waist
the hinge of his aching knee,
the linen-gaitered feet turning
to hooves of mud.

An outstretched arm swings
then dips and dips again into
the coarse grain sack slung
across his hunched shoulder

where the halter rasps the nape
of his raw neck. Big beetroot hands
scatter seed on stony ground,
their moons all ragged and black.

A mercury sky. And his
scissoring bulk fills the frame
forming a large cross with the axis
of oxen dragging their heavy harrow

into the lavender, the rose-flushed dusk,
up at the picture's edge.
Beneath his slouched felt hat
his shrouded face foretells

approaching winter,
the brooding dark. Exhaustion,
waste. Memory of famine runs
atavistic through his veins.

In a ditch a hare pricks
its ears to the wind. A black
scribble of crows writes
hunger across the sky.

Crows over the Wheatfield

I have done with the sun.
Here on these northern
plains wheat fields become
waves, beneath leaden skies
shadows black as dogs
run through the swaying crop.
Long ago I left another country
where the sulphurous sun
hung low over the potato fields.
They called me a madman
because I wanted to be a
true Christian. In Arles
I painted blossom pure as
drifts of Japanese snow.
Now it is upon me again,
this clamped crown.
I who melted gold into
an alchemy of sunflowers
burnished as a lion's mane.
Misfortune must be good
for something . . .
Across the wheat field crows
wheel in a ragged requiem
towards me. My vision
shifts and slides. Three paths
diverge – leading somewhere
going nowhere. My eyes
burn. I cannot hold on.

Path

"They should certainly be killed."

VIRGINIA WOOLF'S *Diary*

Moving aside to draw in the muddy hem of her long
                    tweed coat
against their contaminating touch she lets them
                    pass on the narrow path,
a group of shuffling creatures in single file,
                    a troupe of lunatics
without foreheads or chins, potato faces slit
                    with moony grins   ⁃
that if she does not turn away might hook her in.
                    Mad? Perhaps.
But never a degenerate imbecile like her poor half-sister,
                    spitting and gobbing out her food,
tongue careering faster than a pack
                    of hounds.
But still she feels it coming behind that momentary
                    ecstasy of words:
the jumping pulse, the whirr of wings
                    beating
at the blank window of her mind, can smell the dark
                    cupboard of illness,
its threat of chloral, veronal, paraldehyde,
                    her brain swelling soft as a ripe pear,
the horror of unreason tingling in her veins,
                    and those wild birds singing again,
Greek choruses of Death inside her head.
                    And always the dim
remembrance of that reflected
                    looking-glass shame,

when he ringed her little waist, fat fingers sliding down
                    her unformed frame,
an almost-brother lifting her onto the cold dish-shelf
                    outside the silent
dining-room to feel beneath her flannel skirts.
                    Now
she gathers herself in beneath rough wool,
                    avoids their dribbling stares.
Ahead the path is wet and glazed with leaves
                    where a snail
oozes out its trail of slime.

On Being Given a Voice

Herr Kurtz,   Brussels, April 1902
Chief of the Inner Station,
Belgium Congo.

My dear Love:

This morning there was dew on the lilac; and would you believe
it, outside the Hotel de Ville, the hyacinths are in bloom. So early!
In the market, after church, I purchased a bolt of Brussels lace
to make sheets for our bottom drawer. Now, these long evenings,
I sit in the parchment shadows, edge, with my smallest running
stitch, starched Swiss lawn.

Tonight, my prayers and journal done, I spread, beside
the lamp's orange mantle, as the cone powders and spills
to a dusty heap of grey, the calf-bound atlas upon Grandmère's
rose-wood desk, follow the river's knots and turns, as once by
that summer lake my gloved index traced the furrows of your brow,
into that heart of yellow.

I fear, my love, that my youth is fading. Beneath this black
cretonne I wear till your return lies your gift, the ivory cross,
white and unsullied next to my heart. Each night I dream
strange dreams. As the river laps against the greasy green banks
of my sleep I hear a pulse of drums, see you kneeling naked
– forgive me – skin gleaming

with ointments and oils in the fringed darkness and I am
full fear; though they say that you of all men understand
the savage mind. Now alone in my parlour I close my eyes,
try to banish such brutish scenes, picture your dear face
beaded with the manly sweat of noble toil. I am so proud
to have something to live for.

As ever,
Your Intended

Apprentice Pillar

Rosslyn Chapel, carved 1484

They have eaten the sins of the world
    these eight fishy dragons, scaleless serpents
        with absurdly webbed wings.

Entwined round this stony bole they swim
    its massive girth neither fish nor fowl
        and from their elver jaws vines

coil heavenwards, stripped of speckled leaves,
    flowers, the temptations of fruit,
        like unfledged prayers wafting

into the moss-green light. He dreamt these
    sandstone pleats and waves, a pillar so intricate,
        his Master killed, jealous to see it reaching

towards a rosary of stars, the vault of Virgin lilies,
    stone daisies of Innocence, unnamed flowers
        that open in Adoration of the sun.

I come to it sheltering from a sluice of Scottish rain
    and find an eastern architrave that reads:
        "wine is strong, a King is stronger,

women are stronger, but truth conquers all"
    and wonder if such words apply to me here
        in God's garden where all's right with the world.

It's the second time; lured by loneliness,
    the carved acanthus leaves where Green Men scowl,
        angles blow crumhorns, twang zithers, plonk on lyres.

I could claim it's the art or history; it's easy
    to be seduced by ancient certainties when
        days feel like orchards blighted

by frost or latticed vines pruned bare.
    When all the old familiarities –
        children, lovers with arms as strong

as forest twine braided around the dark
    heartwood have gone, and I am forced back to
        this stripped centre to dream apprentice dreams.

Reckoning

If only I could take you back,
rewind the spool to some lost
afternoon in school, back from
this moment where I sit beside you
as if we might be lovers
or simply friends, our faces close
in front of rows of Curaçao, tequila,
crème de menthe, titled in the bar's
wide glass like two black petals bowed
by summer rain, mother and son,
as your chain smoke curls beside me,
clings to my hair, fills your lungs.
I feel it deep in the pit of me,
a huge fist opening and opening,
this bruising love, as once I felt you,
at first just a thought, growing
and stretching the taut skin of my belly,
its mushroom navel, the web
of silver stretch marks like the trails of snails.
Now I sit beside you, watching you
realise that perhaps what I urged
was right all along;
that that adolescent anger,
that rebellion against buckling down,
books, learning – all you rejected
because it was mine – has led
to this moment, here, together in a bar,
your head in your hands, bowed
like a wet flower on a bent stem
and me helpless to wipe away
the hurt, to make it better,
as you watch your chickens
come painfully home to roost.

Mary

You called me wicked,
claimed I had lain lewdly
in your absence with other
younger men when you saw
my belly swollen, ready
to split open like a ripe fig,
did not know how I had knelt
weak with fear, my hair
like new pressed oil spilt
from a pitcher falling
across my bowed shoulders
onto the dung floor, as the light
was upon me, all milky and sour
as dandelion sap and how
that breath of sulphur had filled
my mouth, a hot metal tongue
making me gag, until my whole
body shuddered as if a bolt
had struck the red ground
up through the roots
of dark yew splitting it in two.
Now my nipples are brown as prunes,
my womb rises like warm dough
as you ask forgiveness, laying
your white head on my stretched
skin, my damp sex, listening
for the heartbeat of God.

Woodcuts

Love is not love until love's vulnerable.

THEODORE ROETHKE

1. Flowers

She wakes into forgetfulness
only her body remembering
the bunch-of-five roses decorating
her white arm, the curve of her bare
shoulder, the tattoo of crimson florets
opening into stamens of black.
Petals of purple where his fingers
had pressed into pale flesh.
And still the smell of him –
flared nostrils, the hot spittle at the edge
of his mouth. Fur and skin and hooves.
And she remembers how that first
time he had called her beautiful,
had with those words wiped away
a father's spilt milk of indifference,
until he too could not bear the taste
of her fear, ripping it from her dark soil
like weeds by the roots.
Now she turns into the tattered
morning, sees across the room
he has unzipped his bull-body:
a small slumped boy with terror on his face.

2. Flood

His sentences spill like rivers across
her wide plains breaking dried banks.

She is drowning in words.
Tides blue as the morning moon rush in

and in, sheets of thawing ice loosen.
Like shattered panes of greenhouse glass.

She tries to escape to the safe hilltops
of herself, to sail over cornfields,

the roofs of houses, attics filled
with dead bees and dust, past fish

dangling like paper lanterns phosphorescent
in the topmost branches of elms.

She would drop anchor with him in a green
meadow but the torrent sweeps on,

as her curved keel grazes the tips of ruined vines
where stringy goats once grazed and dolphins

swim among the pines. She would invite
him to share the quiet places of herself,

but as she gulps for air, he pours in.
The whole briny force of him.

3. Kitchen Dancing

They have closed the door
leaving her to the cracked cornices,
the junk mail on the mat,
hair like graffiti in marbled cakes
of soap, pork chops congealing
in a pool of blood in a polystyrene
pack at the back of the fridge.

She didn't mean to look,
standing in front of the basin,
its polished sentinels of taps –
the foam of her brushed teeth
flecked with threads of crimson –
didn't mean to penetrate that
other brittle gaze, intrude
like a passing stranger's
face on a crowded tube.

Now in the stale morning
among pizza and cold tea-bags,
the debris of other lives,
she strokes her breasts,
her untouched thighs,
throws back her head and
swaying slightly by the sink
slowly stamps out the half-
remembered steps.

4. Morning

Who is this woman
running down the mountain of
morning through the blue-
washed dawn between
the cracked cloches along
puddled paths where dripping
webs of shadow coil
among the glass-house ferns
the spotted orchids
the smeared light speckling
the stagnant pond
where plain carp lurk
beneath black lily pads?

Who is this running woman
hair lifted like straw
by the light wind,
bleached shadow against
the kitchen-garden wall?
Why has she crept
from the snowy fissures,
the steep mountain
of plain starched sheets
into the chill garden carrying
the imprinted breath of him,
the prod of his ice tongue,
his cold glass kiss?

5. Beach

She has turned
from her attic room,
its hairballs of dust,
the secret drawer
of rusted words
and rows of mussel-shells,
the wrapped gull's
faded wing.
Morning strips her bare,
strings debris
along the beach's rim:
rotting necklace
of crab-claw and kelp,
dead bird's beak
oozing its sticky slime,
this picked plastic shoe
broken as a bleached promise.
Now she steps into tides
pale as her dreamings,
beneath wide skirts
nets cod and ling,
bathes her rough sharkskin
in waves insistent
as hands reaching,
reaching
for the very heart of her

Metamorphosis

A Necklace of Tongues

All morning she sits
stitching a necklace of tongues
in her high window,
picking each inert slab

from the shallow porcelain dish
holding its brass-cold weight
muted as a muffled bell
heavy in the dip of her open palm.

Last night snow flakes
melted like kisses,
like salt
on their warm skin,

now her silver needle
pushes through the thick-muscled
root trussing
each glossal silence

with meticulous *petit point.*
If a worm has five hearts,
and an angel none,
how many tongues

does it take to tell lies
about love?
But for now she can only wait,
passing the leaden hour

with herringbone and cross stitch.
Later in front of her mirror of ice
she will lift the cold carrion
like a queen's fringed torque

place it in the soft dip
at the base of her throat,
making visible the muted words,
that wounded song of herself.

Snail Woman

At dawn she picks
mottled spirals
from beneath the lush hostas
chewed overnight to green lace,
fishes them from the white saucer
of treacherous milk, watches
as the grey-tongue bodies glisten
then fizz to mucus
in the trail of cruel salt.
Later she boils the brindled husks
to remove the taste of gritty
garden earth, builds them
now sanitised and cleansed
into a ziggurat,
then slithers inside. In its cool
interiors she grows small, soft,
viscous as putty,
curled in the hidden chambers
tries to understand
the sounds of the world outside.
In the quiet she whispers
into this silence of shells
listening for an echo of her
own breath. She longs
to speak but already
her tongue is turning to slime.

Bird Woman

Words are feathers
on her tongue.
Fledglings struggling to climb
the walls of her chest
clot in her throat.
As she opens her mouth
it fills with a flock
of birds, vomit
of green-black wings.
Song has become the plumage
of starlings, her lips
drawn into a dysphonic O.
For they have cut her silver
cords with the cold
steel of a whetted knife,
hung them like lights
among the rowed vermin:
the jay, the stoat and the crow,
to grow stiff
in the far coppice,
a warning,
on the gamekeeper's wire.

Moss Woman

All night her skin erupts,
her face a sphagnum mask.
Puffballs sprout
from her nostrils
acorns from ears.
Her eyelashes are ferns,
pine needles and twigs poke
from her thicket of wild hair,
dreams snag
like sheep's wool on her spiky briars.
The darkness lures her in
down muddy bridle paths
to a spinney where
she shelters behind
the thick foliage of herself,
her heart in hiding. Here
memories rot,
rank as the fetid stench
of fox,
and silent birds roost
in her deep woods.
Behind her mossy hood
she inhales the reek
of solitude,
dreams of ancient
forests:
of what is concealed
what is wild, mysterious.

Hibernation

They will find me by the smell:
animal scent,
the picked bones and dried droppings

that lead to my lair
snug with stolen goose feathers
and horse hair rescued from spiky briars.

The year is becoming chameleon,
dry leaves curl
brittle as nail parings.

I withdraw, retreat,
the world is growing too cold.
Twigs snap under foot

a glass moon glistens
the thin November frost.
Under my cover I lie

flattening myself
against icy earth
my skin thickening to fur.

Gone to Earth

Death is the mother of beauty; hence from here
Alone, shall come fulfilment of our dreams.
WALLACE STEVENS

Gone to Earth

Finally, one night you slipped in
under my defences,
the chicken wire raised to keep out
foxy dreams – though I had beckoned
before and you had not come.

I found you, in the end, down some
muddy track, fringed with blackberries,
the windows of your car jammed,
each door sealed with gaffer's tape,
the sort of precision you usually
found it hard to muster.

And all around you the blue
was drawing in and in –
wrapping tighter and tighter,
a tourniquet of darkness blotting
out the braille-point stars over
the mounded belly of Salisbury plain,

until you could no longer believe
it would ever end. Then sometime
past midnight, cocooned in a duvet,
you tipped the reclining seat,
turned on the engine and like
a wounded fox, lay down to die . . .

oh my brother, that we might
have held, for a moment, those
duplicitous stars in our joint gaze
before somewhere across the damp
morning fields the dawn rose,
as it would have anyway.

Moon in Andalucia

The church smells of death.
The priest's voice a snowstorm of amplified sound.
Accretions of memory and old women dusty
as veiled Madonnas in nylon-blue.
Calcified slime a green halo rimming the vase.

But in the cemetery death is a carnival,
wedding-cake catacombs glass-edged with chrome,
where silk flowers shimmer bright as Spanish girls' blouses,
sugar-almond saints, a polished room.

And not because I think of you, you come.
Dead-white face in that chapel-of-rest
where death was no carnival but awkward, uncertain,
simply a dream you had to try on.

And in this lime-washed silence I lay out
sugared almonds: heaven-pink, Madonna-blue,
silk flowers bright as Spanish blouses, open the shutters
onto dustless rooms, to jasmine and carnivals of sunlight,
dissolving the tin shadows of a grieving moon.

Books

Amongst "things found"
a vast plastic bag of books
as if, like that boy-king
with his painted peacock-eye
of kohl, you could fill
that metal tomb, that gas-filled car
with seeds of dormant knowledge
like grains of ancient barley that sprout
centuries after the plunder of grave-dark
to equip you for another better life.
Alchemies and knowledge
that had not served, had
failed you here. As if,
as if you could lay down
pearls, gobbets of wisdom
like dates or carved sardonynx,
lapis lazuli set in granulated
beads of gold, rare tinctures or
ointments of myrrh, to be absorbed
through your alabaster skin,
as the night enfolded you,
drew you home across
the dark-green, green-dark
Styx, to where such knowledge
may yield meaning beyond
the hollow howl of words.

Birthday

It returns
inappropriate misnomer
inevitable as the milky cycle of tides,
the salmons' spawning.

I wish I could believe
that what is lost also returns
as I turn my head and see
through the framed window
by the coal fire glowing
in damp November dusk

that small boy in grey shorts,
a belt with serpent clasp,
newspaper spread with
vertebrae of fuselage and wing,
– your Airfix spitfire,
Blue Peter on TV.

And I'd enter that
dim room where the dog
lies snoring by the grate
and the clock ticks on
the red brick mantle,

to sit beside you as you stick
plastic tail to propeller and fin
as we should have knocked home

peg and dowel,
soldered rivet and hasp,
welded words, built bridges
it's now too late to mend.

Loss

It goes on and on
like the blue-veined rivers
that cross and criss-cross maps
or tracks that coil
along rocky coastal paths
where rabbits' droppings
dry in raisin pellets
between gorse and heather
stunted by salt-filled spray.

It goes on and on
like the trace of an owl's
cry from a distant barn,
feathers and fur,
pearl vertebrae of mice
under the rotting straw

endless as the drip
of rain in the high beeches,
the plume of smoke rising
in a coil above the neighbour's
privet, beyond cracked cloches
and stagnant pond, where
leaves gather behind the shed.

Chorus, coda, refrain.

Porth Levan

I have come to the edge,
here where land and ocean meet
things fall away.
Shingle and shale,
the black-pawed cliff
succumb to the sea
its jigsaw bite,
its brute tenacity.

Sand-mottled herring gulls
heave in the wind
and in the harbour mouth
below the wet stone quay
the lobster pots and blue nylon nets,
a lone seal follows
the crab luggers home.

So long after the fact
and you are more with me
now than ever when living –
and like this purple mussel
I carry in my pocket
are both ballast and measure –

as I stand in the wind,
the tide receding in a trail
of feathers and driftwood,
a signature of salt,
as pain lifts like the gull's
ragged wings towards
the horizon where sky
and sea merge grey on grey.

When I go to the cupboard to hang up my coat

I remember it as if
walking round a corner of some forgotten
childhood street and suddenly recollecting
I've been there before and it makes me wonder
why it was you, not me, who didn't hang on,
as I slip back through a fissure in time
to when you were still small, untroubled,
and I stood confused, defiant, as if
offering myself up to them like a delicacy
on a plate for their approval and delectation,
as if my life depended on it,
my face blackened with teenage hurt,
because it felt as though they had punctured
my skin, had rent the membrane of me in two
so that I was leaking, my pure self
seeping out through the snags and gaps
of my imperfection because I knew
I was not what they had dreamed of
or imaged; the good girl, the blonde girl
who would be their ambassador.

And I remember,
though I had forgotten for all these years,
until I reached inside the cupboard,
how I got a pen, an old fashioned fountain,
the sort I used for school to make fair copies,
that spluttered and blotched the lined page
with dark butterflies of Indian ink
and scored on the back wall behind
the laundered steps of school shirts,
the piles of white knickers,
in neat black script, the date and time
of some arbitrary day when,

if I could not make sense of it,
could not bear it any more, I would
wrap myself in darkness, wind myself
back into my own centre coiling inwards
like an insect retracting into its chrysalis
and make it end. But you?
It should never have been you,
the chosen, the prodigal, their only son.

Christmas

I try to imagine
if he came back,
pressing his pale half-forgotten

face against the cold pane,
looking in through shadows
of lamplight and rain

at the smeared glasses, the empty
bottles of wine and fallen needles
of Christmas pine.

The deserted street silent
in December dark, the curtains
at each window drawn tight

to stop the bleeding out of private light
and he watching, as we recycle pain,
wondering why, again and again,

we don't learn love's declensions.
Yet if he stayed a moment longer
he might find, among the smell

of discarded orange rind,
the odour of unmade beds
and drying sheets, of coal dust,

and yellow chrysanthemums
wilting in a jar, a shifting sense
of what has changed –

dilute as a homeopath's dose
invisible in the pale liquid's glass –
into a glimmer of something

precious: like a lost ring,
a pebble, a rusty key,
a question mark of fallen hair.

Journeying North

Room in New York, 1932
after Edward Hopper

Her dress is red.
Her bare arms white as sour cream.
Her hair is malt and softly looped
behind the long arc of her pale neck.
In the half-shadows she scans the page
of her book, her face the colour
of bruised plums, then sighs and turns
towards the lamp which has a shade
the same faded red as her dress.

His shirt is white.
His buttoned waistcoat and knotted tie
are black. He has taken off his jacket
in the heat and opened the window
onto the sticky night.
He sits in a pink velvet chair,
his face inclined towards his newspaper
as sometimes he might incline it
towards a kiss.

Their bowed heads form
a diagonal across the room,
though her chin is titled to the right
and his to the left.
There is nothing between them
except a small round maple-wood table
set with a lace cloth. The table is polished
and shimmers like a lake.
But it is not a lake.

It is simply a table that sits
between them, just as the walls,
which are yellow as illness
are just walls.

Somewhere down the hall
a door slams.

Hotel

In the hush of hidden rooms where a slit
of lamp-light seeps like a half-forgotten memory
beneath her door and hairballs of dust

gather along the mantle by the unmade bed,
she wraps the lonely night about her
in a shawl.

Along buried phone lines the voices of strangers
weep through paper walls bruised as tender skin,
open mouths inhaling rancid dreams.

Above an old man is sleeping his shameless sleep,
while below the nervous girl in a blue dress
unpacks her invisible face in front

of the hostile glass to place it on a shelf
beside the sample soaps,
the sachets of free shampoo.

Outside the wind and rain
are endless. The night lurks,
furtive beneath

the slouching shadows of lamp posts
exhaling its hot breath, as she stands
cheek pressed against the cold pane

watching trams criss-cross the damp city
going somewhere, going nowhere.
Footfalls echo down

silent corridors where pairs of shoes
lie discarded as old loves.
Every journey we make begins and ends

in solitude. Though blood and skin
know that in the secret dark invisible
strangers must breathe in each other's breath.

Journeying North

The hiss of the fan paddles thick air.
        I lay pens,
a ream of paper, corners square,
      on this white desk,
arrange this white room
as if through order
something might be
         .finally achieved
or simply understood.
Sun spills through the Saratogan pines,
      heat deep as a wound,
lifts the voile curtains
like flapping bandages
        on currents of warm air.

Love is never what you expect,
        hidden
like the tiny feathered bones of voles
         disgorged in pellets
in some far field's dark barn:
Nancy, collector of Bakelite
        at antique shows,
who although I made a crush,
        insisted
when all flights were cancelled
       due to summer storms,
I squeeze between her sister, Monica,
         and lardy son,
tester for water impurities on distant farms,
      in the back of their Buick,

the five hour drive to Albany
        along ribbons of wet highway
where motels flashed
        their cut-price seductions;

or Bobo, 300lb ex-hippie,
        the cabby with no teeth
and long blond hair, arms like boiled hams,
        who called me Ma'am
and had once spent nine months in Southern Spain
        high as a kite,
who helped me find my lost bags.

    Later, in the small hours,
        I lay on the raft of my king-size,
flipped the remote between CNN,
        the cookery and chat shows,
as cars revved in the parking lot,
        not knowing how I'd get
        from there to here.

The light
        comes from the east.
This quiet room looks out across terrace and lawns.
    Emotion is born out of habit
        and all this whiteness
        is a form of erasure.

Now I have arrived
    I try and chart where I've been,
where I'm going,
            refigure,
    like fragments of antique glass,
these displaced colours,
        into an approximation
                of something I can understand
Find a dwelling place
                in this pine filled air.

Autumn Rhythm (Number 30)
Jackson Pollock, 1950

It is as if by choosing that chromatic season,
with its slowing harmonies, when light grows thin and pale

on the garden wall, he might find equivalence
to the cacophony of niello swirls, that vortex of duns and pearls

in a veil of morning mist rising across the dew-soaked lawn
or damp twilight gathering like dust in unlit corners.

Perhaps between those interstices of splattered paint,
the smeared ochres and Chinese white, he could smell

wet leaves gathering in gutters, the pulpy stems of dahlias
rotting in terracotta pots or feel the low sun casting shadows

between the frost-bitten leaves of geraniums
yellowing on the slippery planks by the greenhouse door.

Maybe as the nights drew in he tried to push, like a moth
trapped in a vacated room, against the surface of visible light,

afraid that when it was done he would be left
in the dark, that irredeemable, unforgiving dark.

Bat

Between sweat-damp sheets
I lie listening to the hum
of the fan watching
the fat chunk of American moon
hanging above the distant Adirondacks,
in the blue-black night
phosphorescent beyond the rose garden.
My naked body in the heavy heat
accustoming itself to the low breathing
of the narrow bed, to my own touch
hauling myself in like a hand reaching
for someone drowning in deep water,
when as if from the edge of another world –
a flap of inky rag
in the melon moonlight –
it flits in through some forgotten
crack in a drawn screen to appear
silent at the end of my bed
dragging its sooty blacks,
its umbrella wings,
propelling its furry face,
that prick-eared mouse-mask
into my airless room.
I had wanted
skin, muscles, nerves
a heart between these hot sheets,
not this assault from beyond
the fringe of lamp-light;
this gigolo of shadows,
turning my stomach inside out
as he quickens towards me,
tiny white teeth and black cloak,
dark as fresh blood.

Saratogan Morning

Just after dawn a deer and her fawn
broke cover from a thicket of pines
loitering in the clear air on the dew
soaked lawn. The mist was still rising
like mercury, like the feathered
breath from their damp nostrils
or the smoke of distant camp fires,
and for a moment, the deer, her fawn
and I were held in communion
in that hush just before the sun
rose gilding the lake's dull chromes
to pink and ochre and gold
and a small red bird darted across
the clearing like something bursting
in from the rim of this material world.

Meditation

The morning stretches unsullied
   as a sheet grown stiff

with frost between two apple trees.
   Dawn releases its laundered

air through the lungs of pines
   riming the lawn like a green eyelash

heavy with sleep, though the light
   is amniotic, lifting slowly as a fawn struggles

to fluid knees in a hide of bracken.
   I rake myself in like new cut grass

catch the tympani of blue-jays beyond the lake,
   the scent of skunk-piss in the early fog

as seated on this wooden porch I close my eyes,
   breathing against the beat of blood

waiting, watchful
   to welcome myself home.

Sheen

Two suns shimmer on the lake like gilded lily pads
so it is impossible to tell what is lake, sun
or simply gorgeous reflection as the black water
mirrors the aqueous coronae back into the darkening blue.

Everything is still, silent, frozen,
as two dragonflies, like small helicopters,
dart across the surface in a momentary eclipse,
shadow puppets silhouetted against the growing dark.

Even the trees seem to be reaching backwards
into the water, their trunks refracted
between lake and sky into a thousand possibilities.
It would be sublime –

the firefly loch, the stillness, our quiet breathing –
if we could be confident of such a word
in this fractured, unmitigated world.
But you insist, amid all this improbable

loveliness, that what we are looking at
is simply water, that the sun is only the sun,
as if to warn me that this moment can be no more
than itself, must not seep like a stain beyond its edge –

and that like the reeds, the pines,
the mezzotint of sunlight,
we are only matter – simply a man and woman
standing in the opaline dusk, and I acquiesce;

though what I really want to say is:
this is special....
here in the twilight, standing side by side,
as two suns blaze on the surface of a lake.

Toad

It seems to come from somewhere
peripheral so that at first,
as it hops into my field of vision
on the sandy path, I simply think
it is the long grass swaying
among the arsenic shadows
as the darkness winds solitary
and indifferent back into itself
and I bend down on the edge
of the tangled weeds,
the dead leaves, the roots
and hairy ferns and am stopped
by something primordial,
frozen, reptilian: a yellowish
body, bloated, marbled
with black veins like Victorian
end-papers, noduled leather skin
ballooning with fragile breath.
Around me the night wears
a long face and in the hidden houses
sleepers exhale their sulphurous
sighs into the thick night air
and I know that with one careless step
I could crush him, this fat toad.
But alone in this unkind dark,
I am grateful for this small thing
breathing, just quietly breathing.

Study of a Dog
after Francis Bacon

Beyond the date palm
and ribbon of hot sand,
the electric zip of blue sea
and strip of burning highway
where cars black as ants
flow liquid in the heat,
and petrol fumes catch
in the throat like rags,
the midday sun bleaches
colour from the concrete boulevard,
and in a patch of back-street dirt
a brindled dog,
sinews taut, elastic,
turns and turns
in its own shadow,
red-prick tongue hanging
from frilled chops,
chasing its own tail.
Flea ridden, the stink of gutter
clotted in its fetid fur,
it is, behind its black snout
and milk-filmed eye,
behind its helmet of bone
and knowledge of the human,
returning to what is
vicious, taboo, feral,
to what is dangerous.

Digging to Australia

13,000 miles,
            Christmas in summer
            winter in July.
As a child I pressed a shell
to the whorl of my ear
    listening
            for the echo of the sea
as I waited my turn
            to lie
flat against the damp sand
            on the edge
            of that cold English surf
            grit in my groin
my arm disappearing
            to the elbow in the wet
            dark hole,
            digging to Australia.

How did they hang on,
that's what I wanted to know,
dangling upside down on the rim
            of the world,
those topsy-turvy
            koalas and kangaroos,
those fly-walking Down-Under people
poking out from the surface of the earth
like cloves in a Christmas orange?

And what did they dream of
            those other travellers,
the flotsam from our Old World
as they sailed out towards
            the edge

to Van Diemen's, the devil's
own land,
            from the Thames' estuary,
            from Portsmouth,
            on leaking hulks and warships,
double-ironed,
            dressed in coarse slops
to hoick and hack coal,
            burn shells for lime
near aboriginal water holes
            on lands criss-crossed
with sacred dreamings?

            Now
on this far side of the globe
I lie with you
            in winter dark
on the floor of this converted
School House among
            the pale ghosts of children,
beeswax,
            the half-imagined
vestiges of chalk and Indian ink
and wonder
            if this can be enough,
your fingers
            entering and opening me,
as if mining some deep damp dark,
            as once
my arm plunged
into that cold wet hole of sand,
            digging to Australia.

Port Hunter

and will I dream
of this? This rocky shoreline
soon to be blurred
                as if by an invisible curtain of rain
by the fictions of absence
            this ink-stained twilight
                    stippled pink and
                            impossible bronze
these abalone clouds moving
in a reckless choreography
                    over the headland
the smoke stacks and gantries
            the rusting tankers turning
                solid and bulky
in the encroaching dark.

Earlier I stood on the bridge
by the fish factory
watching the men
            barefoot in mud
gutting their catch, throwing
                    purple entrails
            to the gathering pelicans.
It might have been biblical –
        despite the launch, the truck,
                    the concrete pier –
there in the dingy dusk.

The world feels out of reach
        as I walk into deepening blue
            and for a second
                    sense
the separateness of things:

the isolation of each light
flickering across the harbour
   in the salt wind
      from Stockton's suburbs,
the solitary ferry spluttering
        to and fro
across the Hunter,
   the throb of its engine
like the heartbeat of the place
  its passengers
      have come to call home.

I am touched by the melancholy of ships,
their restless
     leaving
and as the bay deepens into black
its calligraphic curve
    beckons towards the light
    and I follow,
uncertain where I'm going
  drawn by an illusion of warmth,
      the clank of freight trains,
  knowing
    I'll never return.

Topographies

He dreams her Himalayan, storms gathering
in her high interiors, rain clouds massing
along the fretwork of her spine. He cannot
climb her icefalls, traverse the sharp ravines
following the dry river bed that winds towards
the deep moist heart. How can he enter her?
Her mossy valleys, her cavernous divinity,
the dark forests of her grievings where rain drips
in tall beeches and wind howls at frozen stars.
How can he touch the elusive bloom of her
as she folds back like a roosting crow's wet wing,
pursue her origin and course when fear blusters
blue and cold from the high hills
covering him with pale flutterings of snow?

Blakeney

A single wooden skiff
    lies beached among the reeds
out beyond the estuary's tidal reach,

layer upon weathered layer
    of paint, a palimpsest in blue
peeling like eczema'd skin,

its hull a bleached
    cage of ribs
rotting in brackish water.

We've come East,
    to where the horizon's
a mere line of pencilled light

and brindled skies squat
    above the fens to mend
what you refuse to,

cannot name, as if in the
    merging of sky, land, reeds,
these beginnings and ends,

something might be permeable
    beneath this waning light.
Four in the afternoon

and the November dusk closes
    in the long horizons, shadows
the corrugated spit of sunlit sand

as we taste the smoke
   of early evening on our lips.
You walk ahead and already

I know you are slipping from me
   as this small trapped craft must have
once slipped from a surf-wet quay.

Oh love, what I want say
   is look; the tide is turning,
turning and refilling these salt pans

as the chambers of an empty heart
   endlessly pour and fill,
pour and spill.

Rope

Sometimes in the small hours
alone now in my too big bed,
I close my eyes and remember
how we made love, you
entering me from behind
as my hands
disappeared in front
of me in a whiteness of pillows,
like a child's buried deep in
a new drift of snow, and
my hair, a dark wave, falling
across the beach of my back,
and how you grabbed it,
the whole length and hank
of it, into a rope so my head
was pulled back, my face
titled upwards like the carved
figure on the prow of a ship
where the wind and salt spray
stung my bare skin,
and how, sometimes, then,
I imagined, years hence,
that you would twine the now
silver-streaked coil, hauling
me in across deep water,
as a fisherman draws in his small
craft to land a shimmering
catch on the stone quay,
slipping the wet rope in a figure
of eight through the heavy
metal ring in a double hitch,
as if securing me fast
as if never wanting to let me go.

Body

Yesterday it was
still there, just as it had been
the day before and all those days
stretching back to that late summer
when I was 11, shut in the gardener's
shed among the seed trays,
the foetid sweetness of apples,
the muddy magazines where
swinging breasts hung like pale pears,
using my father's stolen razor
to shave away those first
question marks of pubic hair.
I wanted pinkness and perfection.
Just as kissing the hotel kitchen-boy
behind the bins that summer,
in Torquay, my parents somewhere
in the bar upstairs, I worried about
the correct trigonometry of teeth
and tongues, or later that first time,
eyes closed, sucking in a concave stomach
convinced myself it was love.

And I remember, too, how it felt
to be turned inside out
like a rubber glove as his head
crowned in the bloody dark,
or how her colic cries made me
harden, brought the milk spurting
into my bluish breasts,
and that moment of hunger
when sleek and wet and wanting
you left a purple trail with your teeth
as you unzipped me entirely

entered and slid in.
And how I touched myself
in those ragged hours until my fingers
smelt of my own damp loneliness.
All these things I remember.
But this morning I woke
without a body and to an end
of broken promises and night starvation,
of waiting like a silly girl for a phone
that doesn't ring. Now there is
only a small stain and nothing,
nothing whatsoever to touch.

Border

Climbing from the bath, all pink-skinned
      and gleaming, she reaches for a towel to wipe
          away the mist from the smeared glass,

and in the pale room's falling light, among
      the brittle shadows of the white tiled room,
          among the lotions and the pills, stands face

to face with a self she hardly knows.
      This is not the woman, half-wrapped
          in a blue towel,

a fraction of her left breast exposed
      she has woken with each morning
          desire dewy on her night breath.

This is the hour of reckoning; the slow descent
      into that other country where alluvial
          flesh thickens criss-crossed with well-worn tracks,

those scars of stubborn hope.
      Now there is only tomorrow's face stripped bare,
          caverns and creases filled with dry dust,

as in the dim light she remembers the curve
      of an outstretched arm once waiting on a crumpled bed;
          a wet mouth opening, that bitter taste of sweat.

Pillow

"Memory
is what you write about,"
you said, as you left me,
as if this new painful vacancy
created by your absence was
really a gift, your going a favour,
as if, without it, I would never
be trying to write a poem,
this poem about your leaving,
trying to describe
the hurt of it,
the wrench-in-the-gut
betrayal of it
now I know you're with
another woman sharing
what you once shared with me,
slipping your fingers inside her,
feeling for her as once you
needed to feel for me,
so that when you came
you cried out and bit
my pillow which I'd
pull away because I loved
the uncontrolled sound of it,
the power of it,
so that, perhaps, I should
be grateful that you've
left and given me this poem
where I try to mould
this hurt into something
more than itself,
this pain which makes me
cry out alone in the dark,

so that I have to muffle
the sound in my pillow like
the shriek of your coming.

Scrabble

The man I learnt to love is
with another woman so
tonight on the balcony
of his friend's friend's
house in *La Borie Basse,*
I sit talking to a man
with an old face
and a young man's body
who's making eyes
at me, whilst inside the lit
window, where his homely wife
of 40 years sets out the *Scrabble*
on a long table.
There are many ways
to be lonely but the way
this man holds my foot
to examine the livid bracelet
of mosquito bites around
my ankle, tells me
that even this transient
intimacy, here under
the Languedoc stars
might fend off, just
for a moment,
that deep terror and offer
a possibility of hope,
like that lit window open
onto the thick night where
in the bright kitchen
his familiar wife moves slowly,
knowing there's no need

to hurry, no need for urgency
as she sets up the game
just beyond the edge
of this unsafe dark.

Gorges de Colombières

Yesterday we climbed
    through chestnuts and pines

to a high pool where a fall tumbled
    from the steep rocks and bathed

under its icy force. And all the while
    I thought of you –

or rather, when I thought
    of you, I tried to picture

that torrent, that cascade
    that had soaked as droplets   as ice

through rifts of limestone and breccia,
    now gushing through my head,

washing away your residue
    like the debris from a dirty room

and as I lay listening
    to that relentless   pouring,

to that curtain of white water
    without beginning   or end

that accepted everything in its wake,
    flowing over it and around it

however misshapen,
    I wanted to become that water,

seeping through crevices
      and cracks, dripping from mossy fissures

into deep pools of netted sunlight.
      I wanted that water's power

to dislodge boulders, rip up
      trees by the root,   to merge

and dissolve,
      to have the strength to be

simply itself, running on   and on
      following its own course to the sea.

Frida

When I wore the cap-sleeved dress
      from Tehuana,
the one with the satin sheen
      the colour of midnight
stitched with pink lilies and twisted vines,
      the one
with the tea-coloured lace at the neck
      and my earrings
of pre-Columbian gold, when I wove braids
      and exotic
scarves around my head,
      you loved me.
For with my wide skirts deep as the green
      shade of primal forests,
where monkeys and Itzcuintli dogs roamed
      in the undergrowth
of my wild hair, I was your motherland
      and despite
an absence of rain, I gave birth
      to prickly pears.

Now summer retreats like a girl
      in a borrowed dress.
Outside my window leaves fall and spin
      and in the spaces where
your voice should be there is only a silence
      like the interval
between a wave rising and falling or
      that moment
at the turn on a flight of dusty stairs
      when a foot reaches
towards another tread.

You opened me like a door
        onto a room of rose light,
now my shattered heart lies trussed in its
        orthopaedic brace,
scar tissue puckered like the red zip of closed lips.
        In the dark of my room
I sit in a man's suit cutting my long hair,
        watching each lock
as it falls, then lifts in the dawn wind like
        a black-headed gull.
I exist in a circle of white unable to face
        the long corridor of morning.
Is there another man in the whole world
        whose belly will fit
to the curve of my broken spine?

Swimmer

I have stepped outside
the world into this catacomb
of sound where voices clatter
on tessellated blue, bounce
against the bone in my head.

Behind the prow of breast-bone
balloon-lungs inflate,
my heart thumps and quickens
against the tepid swell as
I push from the green shallows,
arms shifting the clear weight
of water, pulling my bulk
through the parting wash.

Here I am all otter,
skin sleeked to damp fur,
each hair glistening a mercury
bead of air. I blow whale-bubbles,
snort and splutter, the acid bite
of chlorine etching my throat

as my earth-body elongates,
salmons the flux, feels each
muscle's flex and stretch
against this luminous wall of glass.
and, for a moment, I float
light as air, cleansed.

Page

Nowhere but in this white rectangle
reserved for all that cannot be said,
is solitude so itself.

It erects itself brick by brick
in the gravel footings, the wet mortar that
with brace and strut underpin

the very word it signifies.
Yesterday I swam to the far bank
of this cold Irish lake towards

the heron's nest hidden beneath the willows,
a hundred feet of murky water
plunging down and down to the muddy bed.

On the concrete jetty of the ruined boathouse
something small with teeth had left carcasses
of crayfish like so many discarded thoughts.

To write is a wager with solitude.
What if in the morning light you
glimpse a lavender haze across the lake just

before the sun rises beyond the pines or if
one night swimming in the freezing water you
look down to find the bottom littered with stars?

Notes

1   *Nude in Bathtub*. Bonnard's wife was neurasthenic and suffered with a nervous compulsive disorder, which meant she washed obsessively and had mild agoraphobia. He began this famous painting when she was a young woman and worked on it until her death. In the painting she never appeared to age.

2   *Stereotopica*. A Victorian wooden device, rather like opera glasses or a carnival mask, into which daguerreotypes or early photographs were placed so that they appeared three dimensional.

3   *Darwin's Worms*. Although best known for his work on evolution and the *Origin of the Species*, Darwin was fascinated by the life cycle of worms, which he saw as reflecting the microcosmic pattern of existence. The title is taken from an essay by Adam Phillips.

4   *Crows Over the Wheatfield* was Van Gogh's last known painting.

5   *One Being Given a Voice*. In Conrad's *Heart of Darkness*, his fiancée never speaks. She is the silent, complicit voice of Belgian colonialism.

6   *Apprentice Pillar*. It is said that the Apprentice Pillar in Rosslyn Chapel, carved around 1484, was carved by an apprentice during his master's absence on pilgrimage to Rome. When the master returned he was apparently so jealous at the apprentice's handiwork that he murdered him.

7   *Frida*. The Mexican artist Frida Kahlo 1907–1954 injured her spine in a trolley bus accident as a child, which left her with a permanent disability and caused her to miscarry. She twice married the celebrated communist muralist, Diego Rivera, who was continually unfaithful.

Printed in the United Kingdom
by Lightning Source UK Ltd.
100825UKS00001B/103-114